SPACE EXPLORATION

by Giles Sparrow

A+

Smart Apple Media

Published by Smart Apple Media
P.O. Box 3263, Mankato, Minnesota 56002

Printed in the United States of America at Corporate
Graphics, in North Mankato, Minnesota.

Published by arrangement with the
Watts Publishing Group Ltd., London.

Library of Congress Cataloging-in-Publication Data
Sparrow, Giles, 1970-
  Space exploration / by Giles Sparrow.
    p. cm. -- (Space travel guides)
  Summary: "Presents the life of an astronaut from
take off to surviving, adapting, and working in space
stations. Discusses space travels throughout history,
including the first landing on the Moon, and looks at
future space exploration plans"-- Provided by
publisher.
  Includes index.
  ISBN 978-1-59920-665-3 (lib. bdg.)
  1. Outer space--Exploration--Juvenile literature. 2.
Astronauts--Juvenile literature. I. Title.
  TL793.S688816 2012
  629.45--dc22
                        2010039494

1021
3-2011

9 8 7 6 5 4 3 2 1

Conceived and produced by Tall Tree Ltd
Cartoons: Guy Harvey

Picture credits:
t-top, b-bottom, l-left, r-right, c-center
All images courtesy of NASA, except:
27tr courtesy of Virgin Galactic,
28b Dreamstime.com/Luca Oleastri

Disclaimer
The web site addresses (URLs) included in this book
were valid at the time of going to press. However,
because of the nature of the Internet, it is possible
that some addresses have changed, or sites may
have changed or closed down since publication.
While the author and publisher regret any
inconvenience this may cause to readers, no
responsibility for any such changes can be
accepted by either the author or the publisher.

This book describes a fictional journey into outer
space. It is not possible for humans to travel to
the inner planets with present-day technology.
Readers are invited to use their imaginations to
journey around our solar system.

Words in **bold** are in the glossary on page 30.

Contents

Leaving Earth

In this book, we're taking the trip of a lifetime, exploring what it's like to be an astronaut. We'll learn how spacecrafts leave the Earth and travel out across the **solar system** and what we have learned from space exploration so far. We'll also be taking a look at the challenges and dangers astronauts may face in the future.

BREAKING FREE

The edge of space is just 60 miles (100 km) straight above your head. But Earth's **gravity** is a powerful force that pulls you and everything else down onto its surface and prevents it from leaving. You will have to overcome this gravitational pull first, and for that, you will need a rocket. Once out in space, you will **orbit** the Earth at hundreds of miles per hour in weightless conditions in a completely airless **vacuum**. Looking down, you will be able to see the thin shell of air that surrounds Earth—the atmosphere. This layer of gases supports life on the surface but makes returning from space very difficult. Any object entering the atmosphere at high speeds will be heated to extreme temperatures, and your spacecraft will need heat shields to stop it from being burned to a crisp!

The **Mercury-Atlas 9** *rocket lifted off from Cape Canaveral, Florida, on May 15, 1963. It was piloted by astronaut Gordo Cooper, who was the last American to fly a solo mission to space.*

Despite all these dangers, space is an amazing place and well worth the risk. The ability to put **satellites** in orbit has helped to shape our modern society, and our robot space probes have changed our view of the solar system. One day soon, human colonists on the Moon and other **planets** will open a new stage in the history of the human race.

TRAVELER'S TALES - ESCAPE VELOCITY

Rocket scientists often talk about the Earth's escape velocity, which is the speed you need to achieve in order to entirely escape Earth's gravity. This is roughly 7 miles per second (11.2 km/sec), but you don't need to travel that fast to go into orbit a couple hundred miles up. An orbit is a circular or oval path that one object follows around another, such as a satellite going around the Earth. A spacecraft, such as a space shuttle (see below), needs to be pushed upward with a force or thrust that's strong enough to overcome Earth's gravity and speed the vehicle up enough to go into orbit. In order to put a couple pounds of material into space, a typical rocket has to use 100–200 pounds (50–100 kg) of fuel.

The only practical way of getting into space is by using a chemical rocket. Only these amazing engines have the power to overcome Earth's gravity with their steady, long-lasting force, which starts slowly but builds up to send a spacecraft on its way to orbit and beyond.

BLASTING INTO SPACE

Rockets are engines that work using a principle called action and reaction. The rocket's exhaust escapes in one direction, and the rocket itself is pushed the other way. A rocket produces its exhaust by a process called combustion. This is an explosive chemical reaction in which a fuel (a solid or liquid chemical) burns to produce an expanding cloud of hot gases. Engines on Earth burn their fuel using oxygen from the air around us. Rockets carry tanks containing a chemical called an oxidizer so that they will work in space where there is no air.

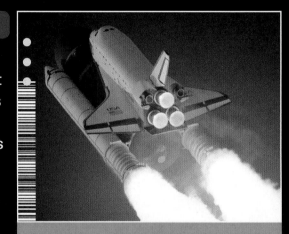

This space shuttle is blasted into orbit by the combined thrust from its three main engines and two huge rocket boosters. Fuel is supplied by the central, rust-colored tank.

TRAVELER'S TALES - ROCKET MAN

Russian and German scientists were among the first to work out many of the principles of rocket-powered spaceflight. The man who put these principles into practice was Robert Goddard, an American professor of physics. Until Goddard's time, rockets had been limited to glorified fireworks that used solid fuels and oxygen from the air. Goddard pioneered liquid-fueled rockets that carried their own oxidizer on board. His ideas were mocked by many people who did not understand how a rocket could work in space, but he proved himself right when his tiny rocket, Nell (shown left), made its first experimental flight in 1926 to a grand height of 43 feet (13 m)! Since Goddard's time, both liquid fuel and solid fuel rockets have made huge advances.

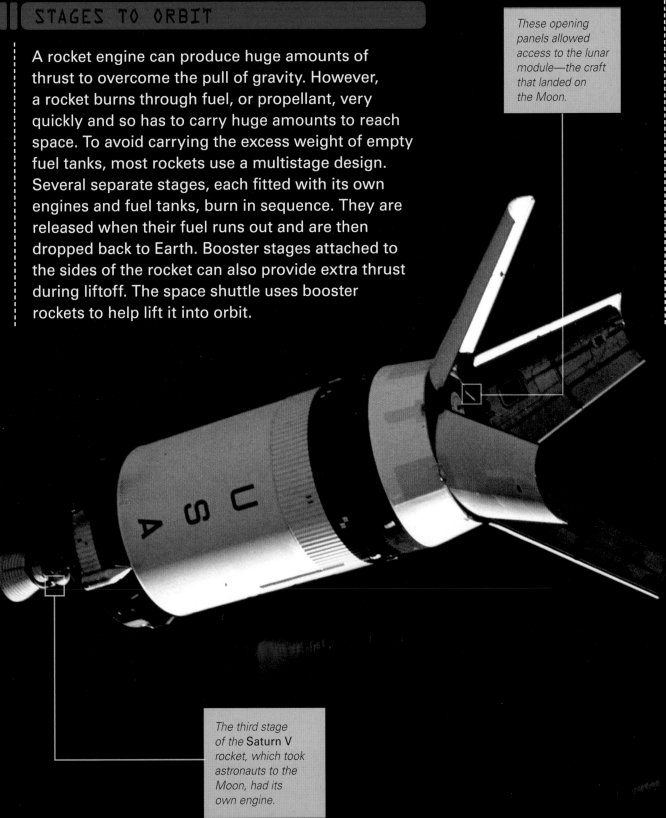

A rocket engine can produce huge amounts of thrust to overcome the pull of gravity. However, a rocket burns through fuel, or propellant, very quickly and so has to carry huge amounts to reach space. To avoid carrying the excess weight of empty fuel tanks, most rockets use a multistage design. Several separate stages, each fitted with its own engines and fuel tanks, burn in sequence. They are released when their fuel runs out and are then dropped back to Earth. Booster stages attached to the sides of the rocket can also provide extra thrust during liftoff. The space shuttle uses booster rockets to help lift it into orbit.

These opening panels allowed access to the lunar module—the craft that landed on the Moon.

The third stage of the **Saturn V** rocket, which took astronauts to the Moon, had its own engine.

Most space launches never really get beyond the pull of Earth's gravity. Instead, they are aimed at putting machines called satellites into orbit. Satellites have a wide range of uses and have revolutionized everyday life since the beginning of the "Space Age" in 1957.

A CLEARER VIEW

Even in a low orbit just 124 miles (200 km) up, a satellite is above Earth's atmosphere. This makes it an ideal viewpoint for studying the universe. The atmosphere is vital to life on Earth, but it is a problem for astronomers as it blurs our views of space. It also blocks out interesting types of radiation (rays like normal light but with more or less energy) given out by objects such as supernovae (exploding stars) and new star systems. Telescopes above the atmosphere can detect these and have added greatly to our knowledge of the cosmos.

*Launched into space by the **Soviet Union** in 1957, Sputnik 1 was the first man-made, Earth-orbiting satellite. It sent back valuable data about Earth's upper atmosphere.*

TRAVELER'S TIPS - HOW TO FIX A SPACE TELESCOPE

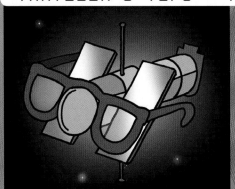

Some satellites are designed to be serviced by astronauts in orbit who will replace broken parts and upgrade others. The most famous of these is the Hubble Space Telescope (see page 9). Launched in 1990, it is still working after two decades and five space shuttle servicing missions. After launch, mission planners found that the telescope had a flaw in its main mirror that left it shortsighted and producing blurry pictures. The first maintenance mission involved installing a set of mirrors that do the same job for the main mirror as a pair of glasses would for a person's eyes!

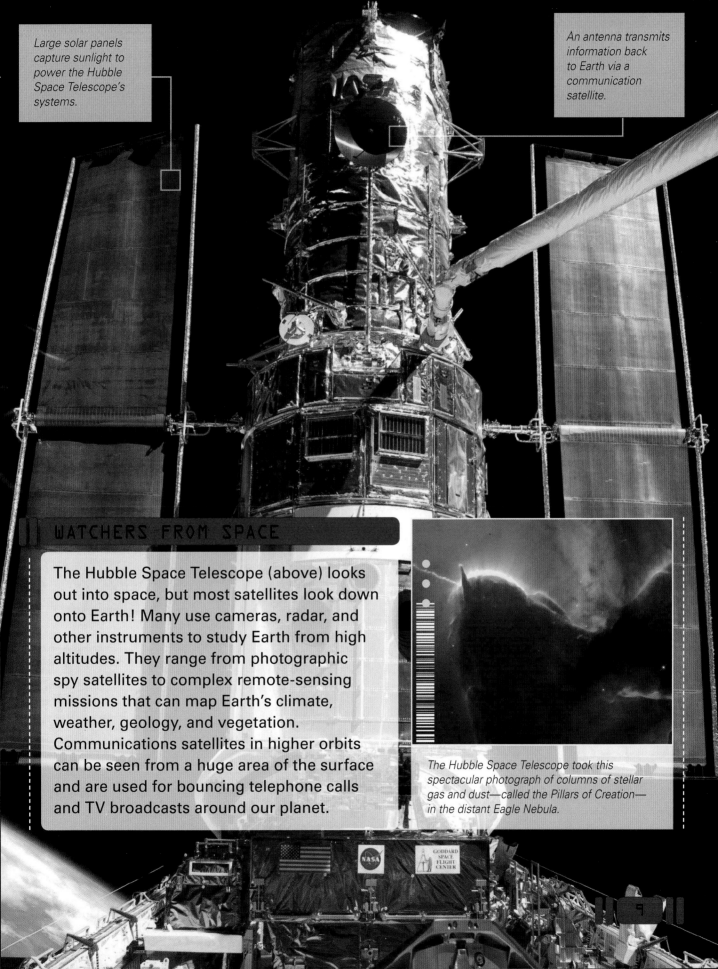

Large solar panels capture sunlight to power the Hubble Space Telescope's systems.

An antenna transmits information back to Earth via a communication satellite.

WATCHERS FROM SPACE

The Hubble Space Telescope (above) looks out into space, but most satellites look down onto Earth! Many use cameras, radar, and other instruments to study Earth from high altitudes. They range from photographic spy satellites to complex remote-sensing missions that can map Earth's climate, weather, geology, and vegetation. Communications satellites in higher orbits can be seen from a huge area of the surface and are used for bouncing telephone calls and TV broadcasts around our planet.

The Hubble Space Telescope took this spectacular photograph of columns of stellar gas and dust—called the Pillars of Creation—in the distant Eagle Nebula.

Humans in Space

To keep astronauts alive, a spacecraft has to protect them from the harsh environment of space and provide air, food, and water. It also needs protective heat shields to survive the re-entry to Earth's atmosphere.

RACE TO SPACE

The first people in space traveled in tiny, cramped capsules. They were launched as part of a **Space Race** between the United States and the Soviet Union (centered on modern Russia) during the 1950s and 1960s. Soviet cosmonaut Yuri Gagarin became the first person to orbit Earth in a 108-minute flight aboard *Vostok 1* on April 12, 1961. American astronaut Alan Shepard flew into space less than a month later, but his *Mercury* spaceship did not stay in orbit.

Yuri Gagarin's flight in 1961 made him world famous, but he never flew into space again. He died in a plane crash on March 27, 1968.

TRAVELER'S TALES - ANIMALS IN SPACE

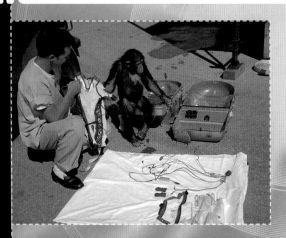

At the start of the Space Race, no one knew whether humans would be able to survive the stresses of spaceflight at all. The Soviet Union put a small dog called Laika in space in 1957 on only the second satellite ever, Sputnik 2, but she died within hours of launch. The U.S. space program used monkeys on early test flights and tested the Mercury spacecraft with two trained chimpanzees called Ham (pictured left, during training) and Enos. Both chimps made it back to Earth safely and showed that they were able to carry out various tasks while orbiting Earth. Today, small animals, such as spiders and fruit flies, occasionally go into space as part of space station experiments into biology and reproduction.

Today, spaceflight is fairly routine and a lot more comfortable. Since the 1980s, the U.S. space agency, **NASA**, has operated a reusable spaceship called the space shuttle, which can carry up to seven astronauts in comfort for two weeks or more. However, this is about to be retired and replaced with a smaller spaceship (see pages 26–27). Russia uses a trusted space capsule design called **Soyuz**, and China uses a similar vehicle. Most human flights today are transfers to and from orbiting space stations (see pages 12–13).

The large, central payload bay of NASA's space shuttle can be used to carry satellites, scientific instruments, or special experiments into Earth's orbit.

Space Stations

A space station is an orbiting science laboratory where astronauts live and work for long periods of time. Since the first stations of the 1970s, these structures have become much larger. Today's huge International Space Station (ISS) covers an area the size of a football field!

A HOME IN ORBIT

Astronauts assemble, extend, and fit out a space station with equipment sent up in unmanned launches. This means that visiting crews can travel to the station in a small spacecraft and do not have to take everything with them. Stations generate power using solar panels and receive more supplies from unmanned ferries. This makes it easier to mount a mission that lasts weeks or months. At the end of their lives, these large structures are de-orbited, ensuring that their remains fall to Earth in the ocean instead of a populated area.

*The United States' first space station, **Skylab**, was in orbit around Earth from 1973 to 1979. Its crews carried out 2,000 hours of experiments.*

TRAVELER'S TIPS - USING THE SPACE TOILET

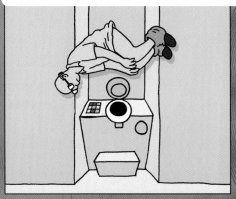

It's the one question everyone asks—how do you go to the bathroom in space? Early astronauts wore a kind of diaper inside their space suits and simply had to let go. That's okay for a flight lasting a few hours, but on a longer mission, that wouldn't be very comfortable! With no gravity to pull stuff downward, everything literally hangs around. Modern space toilets replace the pull of gravity with a current of air that also helps keep the atmosphere inside a spacecraft or station clean. The astronaut gets into position over the seat, holds on to a restraining bar, and lets nature take its course...

The first stations had just a single cylindrical room in which the astronauts had to live, work, and sleep. Since the 1980s, larger stations have been built from a series of modules, each designed for a different function. The solar panels powering the ISS cover a huge area, but the space for the astronauts' crew and work areas is only the size of a medium-sized aircraft—not a lot of room for six people to live in for several months! The ISS involves 15 countries: the United States, Russia, Japan, Canada, Brazil, and 10 member nations of the European Space Agency.

The ISS is made up of a series of interlocking modules, including crew quarters and science labs.

Living with Gravity

On Earth, we're so used to the constant pull of gravity that we more or less ignore it. This is the one thing you can't do in spaceflight. From the ferocious forces that pull you down at liftoff to the difficulties of coping in weightless conditions, gravity is constantly making its presence—or absence—felt.

DEFYING GRAVITY

In order to lift off from Earth, any flying vehicle has to move upward with a force greater than the downward pull of gravity. But in order to reach orbit in the few minutes that it takes to burn up its fuel, a rocket takes this to extremes, pushing upward with many times the force of gravity. The astronauts on board will feel their weight (the downward pull on their bodies) increase by up to three times for as long as a minute. Special training helps them survive without blacking out, and padded couches protect them as much as possible, but it's still a rough ride.

As soon as a spacecraft reaches orbit, the force of the Earth's gravitational pull becomes equal to the force pulling the spacecraft away from the planet. There's nothing extra to make things fall to the floor. This creates a feeling of weightlessness in which there is no up or down, and you can literally fly across a room. Astronauts often suffer from disorientation and space sickness at first, and it can be dangerous when objects do not behave as they do back on Earth.

The walls of the ISS are lined with control panels and scientific equipment, which the astronauts must learn to operate in weightless conditions.

Weightlessness and cramped living conditions make llfe aboard the International Space Station (ISS) a challenging experience. Here, the crewmembers of the ISS have gathered together to take part in a news conference with reporters on Earth.

TRAVELER'S TALES - A RIDE IN THE VOMIT COMET

There are various ways of getting the weightless feeling on Earth. A high-altitude parachute jump can keep you in free fall for a minute or more, and riding a rollercoaster over a drop can give you a few seconds of weightlessness. For the ultimate experience, you can fly in one of the planes NASA uses to train its astronauts. These converted airliners have few seats but do offer a padded interior, which is just as good! As they fly on a steep descending path called a parabola, trainees can go into free fall for up to 25 seconds at a time. It is the only way of making weightlessness in controlled conditions, but there is a downside as many trainees get their first experience of space sickness on board. Little wonder these planes are nicknamed "Vomit Comets!"

Working in Orbit

Astronauts don't just go into space for the fun of it. They usually have a job to do when they get there! Whether it is a laboratory experiment or an orbital construction project, most people go through months of training to be ready for the tasks ahead of them.

SCIENCE IN ORBIT

Working in space, even a low orbit just above Earth's atmosphere, has two big advantages for scientists. Firstly, it's a near-perfect, airless vacuum—something that's hard to create on Earth. Secondly, there's effectively no gravity. This creates opportunities for scientists to study how various chemicals and materials form in these conditions. They can apply what they learn to improve the way things are made back on Earth.

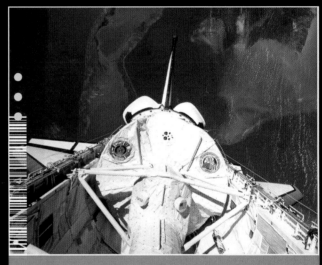

Scientists carried out a wide range of experiments in Spacelab, a laboratory module carried into space in the payload bay of the space shuttle.

TRAVELER'S TIPS - HOW TO PUT ON A SPACE SUIT

Getting into a space suit can be a tricky business. Since it may be all that is protecting you from a variety of forms of sudden death, it is not something you should rush. Some suit designs have several parts, such as a jumpsuit that you climb into and zip up before attaching shoes, gloves, and a helmet and locking them into place with seals. Others are simple, bulky hard shells. Everything's joined into one unit that has a hinge at the waist. You climb into the pants first and then pull the rest up and over your head before sealing the midriff. Once your suit is finally on, you will still need to attach a life-support backpack with various color-coded hoses to provide it with air, cooling systems, and electricity.

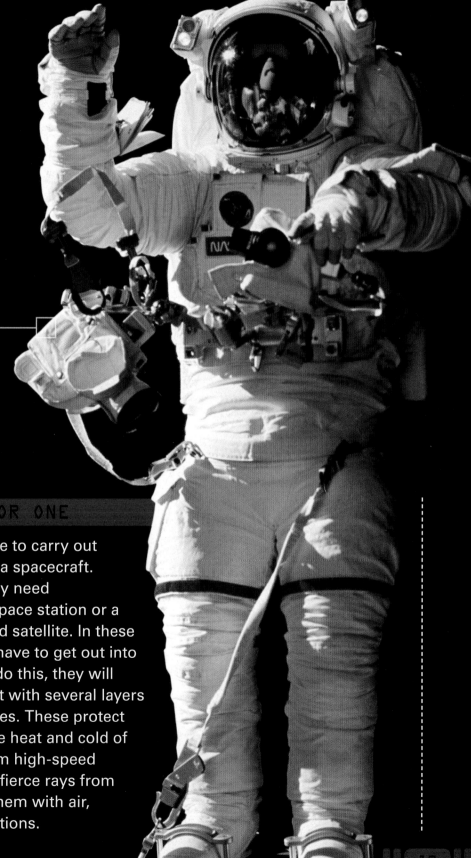

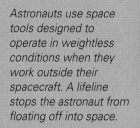
A SPACESHIP FOR ONE

It is not always possible to carry out every task from inside a spacecraft. Sometimes a cable may need connecting on a new space station or a part replacing on an old satellite. In these situations, astronauts have to get out into space themselves. To do this, they will wear a bulky space suit with several layers plus a helmet and gloves. These protect the astronauts from the heat and cold of space, shield them from high-speed fragments of dust and fierce rays from the Sun, and provide them with air, water, and communications.

Space is a dangerous place. Air leaks, fires, and impacts from chunks of space rock all pose a threat. There are also risks to the human body just from being in space. Fortunately, you can do something about many of these.

KEEPING FIT

On Earth, our muscles and bones are constantly working just to keep us upright against the pull of gravity. In the weightlessness of space, they get lazy. Muscles become weaker through lack of exercise, and our bodies forget to reinforce bones with the calcium they need for strength. Even the cells that carry oxygen around our blood get out of condition! In order to return to Earth in a healthy condition, regular exercise and a variety of medicines are a must for all long-stay astronauts.

To keep themselves fit and make sure their muscles stay toned up, astronauts aboard the International Space Station exercise using a running machine.

TRAVELER'S TIPS - MICROMETEORITES

Space is full of junk. The solar system is filled with rocks and dust left over after the planets formed, and the region around Earth is crowded with trash left behind by our exploration. Apart from the functioning and shut-down satellites, there are old rocket stages, mislaid tools, and countless nuts, bolts, and flecks of paint. Collisions with space junk or small rock particles called micrometeorites can be a problem. This picture shows a hole punched into a space shuttle by a micrometeorite. Fortunately, there's still a lot of empty space around Earth, so collisions are rare. But they do happen, and you better hope your spacecraft is equipped to cope with them!

There are many other hazards associated with space flight and some are difficult to foresee. One danger is the increased exposure to space radiation, which we are normally shielded from on Earth. Some astronauts find the cramped conditions or sheer isolation difficult to cope with. They may end up fighting among themselves or become withdrawn and depressed. And the dangers we do not know about could be even worse. The *Apollo 11* astronauts—the first humans to walk on the Moon—were kept in quarantine for 21 days after their return just in case they had brought back any unknown space diseases. Luckily, they hadn't.

*Safely secured in a quarantine chamber, the **Apollo 11** crew was greeted by U.S. President Nixon.*

HORNET + 3

Earth's Moon is about 250,000 miles (400,000 km) away. It is the farthest humans have traveled into space and the only other world we've set foot on so far. To achieve this required a huge effort, budget, and the work of thousands of people.

ROCKET TO THE MOON

In 1961, U.S. President John F. Kennedy set NASA on the task of landing a man on the Moon before the end of the decade. This mission, which became known as the Apollo program, was to be the final chapter in the Space Race between America and the Soviet Union and consumed huge amounts of resources. The most impressive symbol of this project was the enormous *Saturn V* rocket, 364 feet (111 m) tall and built to send the Apollo spacecraft on its way to the Moon.

*The **Saturn V** was a three-stage spacecraft. Each stage contained its own rocket engine. The stages were discarded once their rocket fuel was exhausted.*

*Held upright by a launch tower, the **Saturn V** was moved very slowly on a mobile platform from an assembly building to the launch area. A lift carried the astronauts up the tower to the crew capsule at the top of the rocket.*

After launching into Earth's orbit, a final burn of the *Saturn V*'s third stage sent the Apollo spacecraft on its way to the Moon. The Apollo vehicle had three parts: the Command Module, or crew capsule, the Service Module that supplied it with air, water, and power, and the spider-legged Lunar Module that would make the actual landing. After a three-day journey, the Service Module's engines fired to put Apollo in orbit around the Moon. Two astronauts then descended to the surface in the Lunar Module, while a third stayed in orbit on the Command Module.

TRAVELER'S TALES – APOLLO 13

Six Apollo missions landed on the Moon between 1969 and 1972, but the crew of another was lucky just to get back to Earth alive. Apollo 13 *suffered a fuel explosion on the way to the Moon that left its Service Module crippled. With limited power and failing life support in the Command Module (the crew capsule), NASA engineers at Mission Control came up with a desperate plan. The three astronauts, Jim Lovell, Jack Swigert, and Fred Haise, would transfer into the cramped Lunar Module and use it like a lifeboat to keep them alive for four days as they looped around the Moon before traveling back to Earth. The world watched as they then had to restart the Command Module before separating from the Lunar and Service Modules to descend back to Earth.* Apollo 13 *may not have landed on the Moon, but the crew's safe return was one of NASA's greatest triumphs.*

After safely splashing down in the Pacific Ocean, the **Apollo 13** *Command Module was winched aboard a U.S. navy aircraft carrier (above left). The spacecraft crew (above right) were hailed as national heroes.*

On the Moon

On July 20, 1969, Neil Armstrong and Buzz Aldrin became the first humans to land on the Moon. They spent less than a day there, including a two-and-a-half-hour moonwalk. Later Apollo missions spent up to three days on the Moon, carrying out a range of experiments.

WALKING ON THE MOON

Stepping onto the Moon's surface is a strange experience. The low gravity gives you just one-sixth of your Earth weight, meaning you can leap high off the ground and cover huge distances at a single bound. You just need to think about how to stop! The ground is covered in a fine, powdery gray dust that sticks to everything and reflects glaring bright sunlight in the day. And, of course, there's no air for you to breathe!

Earth rises above the Moon's horizon in this photograph taken from the **Apollo 11 Command Module,** *which remained in orbit around the Moon as Armstrong and Aldrin descended to the surface.*

TRAVELER'S TIPS - DRIVING ON THE MOON

Apollos 15, 16, and 17 carried a special Moon buggy called the Lunar Roving Vehicle (LRV). It cost $38 million to develop and could reach a top speed of 11 mph (18 km/h). Four independently driven wheels got the vehicle out of dust-drifts and enabled it to bounce over small rocks, but concealed craters and larger boulders were a problem. Size and distance are hard to judge on the Moon. Its small size means the horizon is closer than you think, and the lack of atmosphere means there are crystal-clear views of even faraway objects. A small nearby rock may turn out to be a distant boulder the size of a house!

Between 1969 and 1972, six Apollo landers came down on different areas of the Moon's surface. Their main job was to collect rock and soil samples that would help geologists on Earth piece together the Moon's history. The three later missions were equipped with Lunar Roving Vehicles, which helped them cover much larger distances. Experiments included revisiting old robot landers to see how they had lasted, sending shockwaves through the Moon's surface, and setting up devices to listen for moonquakes. It wasn't all hard work, though. *Apollo 14* commander Alan Shepard became the Moon's first golfer, using an improvised club and a ball!

NASA astronaut Eugene Cernan test-drives the Apollo 17 Lunar Roving Vehicle *on the Moon's surface in 1972, shortly after unloading the vehicle from the Lunar Module.*

Probing the Planets

While humans have so far only visited the Moon, robot space probes have explored nearly every corner of the solar system. Cheaper and less dangerous than manned missions, these probes have visited all the major planets and many moons, comets, and asteroids.

MEETING THE NEIGHBORS

The most popular targets for probes are planets nearest to Earth: Venus and Mars. Attempts to land on Venus are doomed to destruction because of its baking, acidic atmosphere, but orbiter probes can circle the planet and use radar to peer through its dense clouds. Mars is more welcoming, and a host of missions have now orbited, landed on, and even driven across its surface. Other missions have visited Mercury (the nearest planet to the Sun) and comets and asteroids passing through our region of the solar system.

The Mars Rover **Spirit** landed on Mars on January 4, 2004. It has sent back a great deal of information about Mars's surface features.

TRAVELER'S TIPS - INTO THE DARKNESS

Any spacecraft will face a lot of challenges exploring the outer solar system. Beyond Mars, the Sun gets too weak for solar cells to work efficiently, so you need another power source. Space probes can use the heat from radioactive elements, but a human mission will need a nuclear power plant. Journeys will take years, and astronauts will have to take lots of supplies and spend a very long time in space. Radio signals take a few minutes to travel from Earth to Mars, but farther out, they take hours to go back and forth. With no hotline to Mission Control, the crew will have to make its own decisions in a crisis.

Launched by NASA in 1989, the **Galileo** space probe was sent to study Jupiter and its moons. After a six-year journey, it became the first spacecraft to orbit Jupiter.

THE OUTER PLANETS

Only a few missions have ventured beyond Mars to visit the giant planets of the outer solar system. *Voyager 2*, launched in 1977, visited all four in turn— Jupiter, Saturn, Uranus, and Neptune— sending back breathtaking images. More recently, Jupiter and Saturn have been visited by probes called *Galileo* and *Cassini*. And even though it's not really a planet, tiny Pluto hasn't been forgotten. A mission called *New Horizons* is speeding toward it and is due to arrive in 2015.

Voyager 2 is the only spacecraft to have visited the outer planets Uranus and Neptune. The probe is now heading into interstellar space.

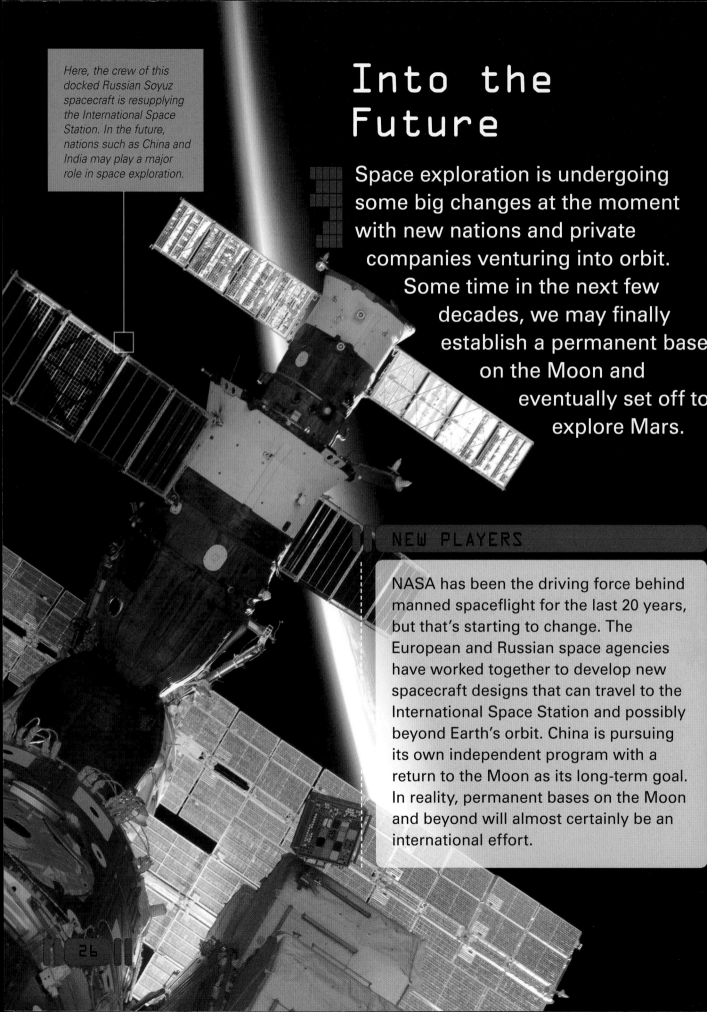

Here, the crew of this docked Russian Soyuz spacecraft is resupplying the International Space Station. In the future, nations such as China and India may play a major role in space exploration.

Into the Future

Space exploration is undergoing some big changes at the moment with new nations and private companies venturing into orbit. Some time in the next few decades, we may finally establish a permanent base on the Moon and eventually set off to explore Mars.

NEW PLAYERS

NASA has been the driving force behind manned spaceflight for the last 20 years, but that's starting to change. The European and Russian space agencies have worked together to develop new spacecraft designs that can travel to the International Space Station and possibly beyond Earth's orbit. China is pursuing its own independent program with a return to the Moon as its long-term goal. In reality, permanent bases on the Moon and beyond will almost certainly be an international effort.

COMMERCIAL SPACEFLIGHT

While the first 50 years of space exploration were run by government space agencies, the future may be driven by private companies. In 2004, Virgin Galactic's *SpaceShipOne* became the first privately built vehicle to reach space. The company will soon begin offering passenger trips with the same technology. While the Virgin flights won't reach orbit, other space companies are working to develop new launch vehicles and spacecrafts to supply the International Space Station.

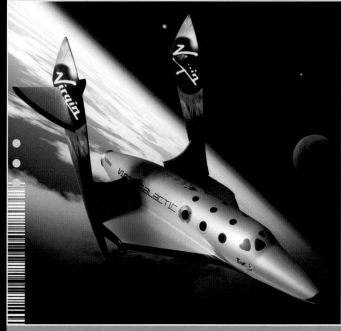

Virgin Galactic's spacecraft will carry up to six passengers to the edge of space. At a height of 68 miles (110 km), passengers will be able to see the curvature of the Earth.

TRAVELER'S TALES - THE MOON AND MARS

In 2004, President George W. Bush asked NASA to plan a strategy for returning to the Moon. The project was to be called Constellation, and it got as far as a test launch of a new rocket, the Ares X-1, in 2009 before budget cuts forced its cancellation. NASA is now looking at other options, but a heavyweight launch vehicle capable of going beyond low orbit is still a priority. The obvious targets for exploration are the Moon and Mars. Both are nearby in interplanetary terms, and space probes have revealed that each has substantial deposits of ice either on the surface or buried in the soil. This could provide water and oxygen to breathe. It could even be used to create fuel for power plants or to power propulsion systems for the return to Earth or trips farther out into the solar system.

Future astronauts exploring the surface of Mars would use specially designed scientific equipment to carry out research on the Martian soil, rocks, and atmosphere.

Beyond the Solar System

One day, humans will want to journey beyond the solar system to visit other stars, establish colonies, and spread out across the galaxy, perhaps meeting alien civilizations along the way. But interstellar travel is a huge challenge compared to solar system exploration.

INTO DEEP SPACE

Getting to even the nearest stars at the speed of an Apollo spaceship would take 100,000 years or more. Even if our technology improves greatly, most interstellar journeys will still probably take centuries. There are only two likely solutions to this problem. One would involve huge, self-supporting **colony ships** whose crews would go through many generations on the way to their destination. The other would involve suspended animation, which would see a single crew put into frozen hibernation for much of their journey before waking up near the end of the voyage.

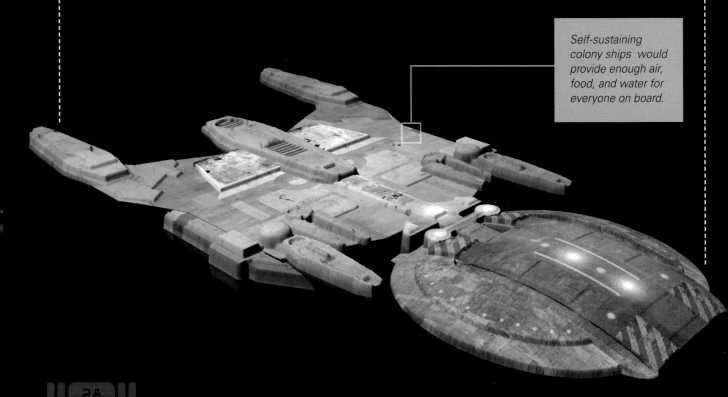

Self-sustaining colony ships would provide enough air, food, and water for everyone on board.

Although they are useful, chemical rockets are quite inefficient. Some experimental spacecrafts have already begun to use new technologies to drive them forward, and these could be the key to high-speed interstellar travel. They range from ion engines, which gradually build up to very high speeds and use very little fuel, to solar sails, which need no fuel at all, relying instead on the weak push of the Sun's rays. Some physicists hope that a scientific breakthrough might allow us to use **wormholes** in space for instant travel across the universe.

Ion drives are very fuel-efficient, but they are not as powerful as conventional chemical rockets. Scientists are currently developing new engine systems that can generate greater thrust.

Ion drives fire out beams of electrically charged atoms (ions) to push a spacecraft along.

TRAVELER'S TIPS - SAYING HELLO TO ALIENS

If we do ever meet aliens, how do we talk to them? Scientists believe the best way to communicate face to face would be using pictures (assuming the aliens have a sense similar to sight). If we are limited to trading radio signals, the easiest way to talk would be the universal language of mathematics. But even everyday math makes human assumptions. Our numbering system is based on our ten fingers. However, binary numbers—the system of 1s and 0s used by computers —are the simplest form of counting possible. Any intelligent alien civilization would probably understand them.

Glossary

Colony ship
A spaceship that would travel to the stars over hundreds of years with many generations being raised on board

Gravity
The force of attraction that astronomical bodies exert on each other as a result of their masses; The more massive they are, the stronger the gravitational force.

NASA
The National Aeronautical and Space Administration, an agency of the U.S. government responsible for the nation's space program

Orbit
The curved path of a physical object in outer space, such as a moon, planet, star, or asteroid (a space rock), around another as a result of strong gravitational attraction

Planet
An object that follows its own orbit around a star and is massive enough to be rounded into a spherical shape by its own gravity

Satellite
A physical object in space orbiting a planet or star; Manmade satellites include devices placed in orbit around the Earth to relay scientific or communications data.

Solar system
The Sun together with the eight planets—Mercury, Venus, Earth, Mars, Jupiter, Saturn, Uranus, and Neptune—and the other astronomical bodies that orbit it

Soviet Union
A former country in eastern Europe and northern Asia; Established in 1922 and officially dissolved in 1991, it was centered around Russia and included 14 other states.

Soyuz
A series of spacecrafts designed for the Soviet space program, consisting of an orbital module, a re-entry module, and a service module

Space Race
An informal competition between the United States and the Soviet Union from 1957 to 1975 as each side tried to match or better the other's achievements in exploring outer space

Vacuum
A volume of space that is essentially empty of matter

Wormhole
A theoretical tunnel through space that allows quick travel from one part of the universe to another

Resources

BOOKS

Exploring Space
Earth and Space Science
by Robert Snedden
(Raintree, 2010)

Man Walks on the Moon
Days of Change
by Valerie Bodden
(Creative Education, 2010)

Robots in Space
Robot World
by Steve Parker
(Amicus, 2011)

Voyage through Space
Space Guides
by Peter Grego
(QEB Publishing, 2008)

QUICK QUIZ

Here are three quick-fire questions to test your spaceflight knowledge. (Answers at the bottom) Good luck!

1. Which was the first on the Moon? Was it:
a) *Apollo 13*
b) *Apollo 11*
c) *Apollo 15*

2. What is the name of the first spacecraft to orbit Jupiter? Is it:
a) *Galileo*
b) *Spirit*
c) *Cassini*

3. What is Voyager? Is it:
a) a star
b) a space rocket
c) a space probe

WEB SITES

www.universetoday.com
Space exploration and astronomy news brought to you from around the Internet

www.nasa.gov/audience/forstudents
Scientists from NASA answer your questions on the solar system and the universe.

www.pluto.jhuapl.edu
The latest reports on NASA's Pluto-Kuiper Belt space probe mission, due to encounter Pluto in July 2015

www.spaceplace.nasa.gov/en/kids
Out-of-this-world space puzzles, quizzes, and activities to test your knowledge

www.space.com
Information on everything to do with space—satellites, stars, astronomy, the Sun, planets, NASA, and more

www.sciencewithme.com
A variety of resources about space exploration and spaceflight; Includes many interactive and 3D animated views

Quiz Answers: 1. b 2. a 3. c

Index